AGE DON'T MAKE YOU GROWN —

YOUR DECISIONS DO

A Blueprint for Stability, Healing, and Legacy

Dedication

First and foremost, I thank my Lord and Savior, Jesus Christ, for always protecting me—especially during the moments when He was protecting me from myself. His grace, mercy, and guidance carried me through seasons I didn't always understand, but now deeply appreciate.

I dedicate this book to my children—Larry, LaChelle, and LaShai. You three pushed me to grow, mature, and become the person I am today. Watching you grow gave my life deeper purpose and reminded me daily that my decisions matter far beyond myself.

To my older sisters—Nina, Lavonda, and Kitty—thank you for protecting me when I couldn't protect myself. Your strength, loyalty, and love covered me during seasons when I was still learning how to stand on my own.

To my youth coaches and adult mentors—Coach Terrell, Ken, and Myesha—thank you for seeing something in me before I could fully see it in myself. Your guidance, discipline, and belief helped shape my foundation and direction.

To my mother, thank you for doing the best you could with the cards you were dealt and for pushing through struggles that many will never understand. Your resilience planted seeds in me that still grow today.

And to my true friends—those who served as my sounding board, counselors, and support system when I needed it most—thank you for standing with me in both silence and struggle. This book carries pieces of all of you.

About the Author

Larry D. Wilcox is a Cleveland native, U.S. Army combat veteran, community leader, and nationally recognized youth mentor. His life's work centers on helping young people and families build stability, discipline, and purpose in the face of adversity.

After growing up in poverty and navigating early academic struggles, Larry found direction through mentorship, discipline, and military service. He served nearly eight years in the United States Army, completing combat and overseas deployments that shaped his leadership, resilience, and commitment to service. Following his honorable discharge, Larry dedicated his life to community development and youth empowerment.

He is the founder of *Turn It Up Leadership Group*, an organization focused on leadership development, social-emotional learning, and life-stability programs for underserved youth. Larry currently serves as a Recreation Manager for the City of Cleveland and is completing his Master of Social Work at Cleveland State University, where he also works as a Care Management intern in the Vikes

CARE Office supporting students facing housing, mental health, and life challenges.

Recognized for his service and leadership, Larry has received numerous community and academic honors, including Cleveland State University's Student Veteran of the Year Award. Through his speaking, mentorship, and writing, Larry equips individuals to make intentional decisions, break generational cycles, and build lives of purpose, discipline, and legacy.

Introduction

Age Don't Make You Grown — Your Decisions Do is not a motivational book. It is a life blueprint for anyone who grew up without a map. Written by U.S. Army combat veteran, community leader, and youth mentor Larry D. Wilcox, this powerful manual delivers real-life truth, discipline systems, and healing strategies for building stability, purpose, and legacy.

Through raw personal stories, practical decision frameworks, and step-by-step life structure tools, Wilcox shows how daily choices—not age, talent, or luck—determine your future. Readers are challenged to break destructive cycles, rebuild their mindset, protect their name, and create systems that produce peace, discipline, and generational change.

Whether you are navigating adolescence, rebuilding after trauma, transitioning from military service, or searching for purpose, this book provides a clear roadmap to stability, confidence, and leadership. This is not just a book—it is a blueprint for becoming the person your future deserves.

CHAPTER 1

PEOPLE GET OLDER. LEADERS GET BUILT.

There are people who get older.
And there are leaders who get built.

They are not the same.

I know, because I was both.

I grew up in poverty. No blueprint. No roadmap. No real example of what stability, discipline, and structure actually looked like. I had heart, but heart without structure still bleeds. I had potential, but potential without direction still drifts.

Nobody sat me down and said,
"Here's how you build your life."
"Here's how you protect your future."
"Here's how you keep your name clean."
So I learned in the streets. And the streets don't teach — they test.

I watched teenagers turn 18 and think they were grown.
I watched adults turn 40 and still live in survival mode.

And I almost became one of them.

THE MOMENT THAT SPLIT MY LIFE IN TWO

There was a point where my life could've gone either way.

College wasn't working.
Money was tight.
Pressure was heavy.
The streets were loud.
The system was waiting.

I wasn't lazy — I was unstructured.

And that's when a man who wasn't even family stepped in.
My basketball coach didn't just teach me how to run plays
— he taught me how to run my life.

He didn't just say "work hard."
He said:

- Show up early

- Keep your word

- Respect your name

- Train your body

- Train your mind

- Choose your circle

That was the first time I learned:

Growth is not a birthday. It is a decision system.

WHAT BUILDING A LEADER ACTUALLY MEANS

A drifter reacts.

A leader structures.

A drifter feels.

A leader decides.

A drifter survives.

A leader stabilizes.

Your life is not built on your feelings.

It's built on your daily decisions.

Your sleep habits.

Your diet.

Your money moves.

Your circle.

Your discipline.

Your boundaries.

Your grind.

These are not "adult things."
These are **protection systems.**

Because the world does not break down strong people —
It breaks down unstructured people.

MY FIRST REAL DECISION

The first real decision I ever made was this:

I chose structure over chaos.

I chose the military over the streets.
I chose discipline over comfort.
I chose pain with purpose over pain with no direction.

The military didn't just give me a job.
It gave me a spine.

It taught me:

- Show up tired
- Work when it hurts
- Finish what you start
- Protect your people
- Keep your word
- Carry weight
- Stay accountable

That structure saved my life.

Not because I became perfect —
But because I became **directed.**

THE REAL TEACHING

You do not drift into greatness.
You do not luck your way into stability.
You do not feel your way into leadership.

You **decide** your way there.

And you make that decision **daily.**

REFLECTION

Ask yourself:

• Who am I becoming by my habits?

• If someone copies my life, will they be protected or exposed?

• Is my life structured… or just surviving?

<u>Writing space:</u>

_____

_____

_____

_____

_____

_____

_____

_____

_____

_____

_____

_____

_____

_____

ACTION CHALLENGE

Starting today:

Wake up earlier

Move your body daily

Track your money

Audit your circle

Protect your name

Choose one discipline and master it

Not to look tough.

To **be unbreakable.**

<u>Writing space:</u>

LEGACY KEYS

• Structure beats motivation

• Decisions shape destiny

- Growth is built, not granted
- Your discipline is your shield
- Your life is someone else's blueprint

CHAPTER 2

YOUR DECISIONS CREATE YOUR DIRECTION

Nobody wakes up in a bad life by accident.

Nobody "just ends up" broke, unstable, addicted, incarcerated, burned out, or emotionally numb.

They arrive there one decision at a time.

I've watched it happen to people I love.
And I've watched myself almost become one of them.

Your life does not move randomly.
It moves in the direction of your daily choices.

Not your intentions.
Not your dreams.
Not your prayers.

Your **decisions.**

THE FORK IN THE ROAD

There was a season in my life where everything was loud.

Loud friends.
Loud streets.
Loud pressure.
Loud temptation.
Loud distractions.

I was standing at a fork in the road — and I didn't even know it.

One side led to structure, discipline, and purpose.
The other side led to chaos, fast money, and temporary validation.

Both looked real.
Both felt possible.

But only one was safe.

I didn't choose the right path because I felt strong.
I chose it because I felt tired of surviving.

And that decision redirected my entire bloodline.

DECISIONS ARE DOORS

Every decision opens a door.

Some doors lead to peace.

Some lead to probation.

Some lead to stability.

Some lead to survival mode.

You don't fall into traps — you walk into them through unguarded decisions.

- Who you answer calls from
- Where you hang when nobody is watching
- How you spend your money
- What you feed your mind
- What you tolerate
- What you repeat

These are doors.

And doors shape destinies.

WHY PEOPLE STAY STUCK

People don't stay stuck because they're weak.

They stay stuck because they keep making **familiar decisions** instead of **forward decisions.**

Familiar feels safe.
Forward feels uncomfortable.

But growth always requires discomfort.

MY TURNING POINT

My turning point wasn't a speech.
It wasn't a sermon.
It wasn't a miracle.

It was a decision.

I decided to stop waiting for motivation and start building systems.

Wake-up times.
Workout routines.
Education goals.
Money tracking.
Circle boundaries.
Spiritual discipline.

Those systems saved me when emotions failed me.

REFLECTION

Ask yourself:

- What decision do I repeat that keeps me stuck?
- What decision would move me forward immediately?
- Who do I need to stop listening to?

<u>Writing space:</u>

_____

_____

_____

_____

_____

_____

_____

_____

_____

_____

_____

_____

ACTION CHALLENGE

Starting today:

Choose one habit to cut.

Choose one habit to build.

Protect your time.

Protect your circle.

Protect your future.

Your next decision is a door.

Choose wisely.

Writing space:

_____

_____

_____

_____

_____

LEGACY KEYS

• Decisions are destiny

• Familiar kills futures

• Systems protect success

- Discomfort creates direction
- Your choices shape generations

CHAPTER 3

PAIN DOESN'T EXCUSE BAD DECISIONS

Your pain is real.

Your trauma is real.

Your losses are real.

Your scars are real.

But your pain cannot drive your life.

Because pain that drives eventually crashes everything.

I know this personally.

THE COST OF UNPROCESSED PAIN

I served in combat.

I watched brothers bleed.

I buried friends.

I lived under rocket alarms and uncertainty.

I normalized danger.

And when I came home, the war didn't stop — it just changed locations.

The nightmares.
The anger.
The isolation.
The drinking.
The emotional shutdown.

That wasn't weakness.
That was unprocessed trauma.

But here's the truth most people don't hear:

Pain explains behavior —
It does not excuse self-destruction.

HOW TRAUMA HIDES

Trauma doesn't always cry.
Sometimes it drinks.
Sometimes it sleeps all day.
Sometimes it works nonstop.
Sometimes it isolates.
Sometimes it self-sabotages relationships.

I didn't realize I was bleeding internally while I was still functioning externally.

But functioning is not healing.

ACCOUNTABILITY SAVED ME

Healing didn't start when I felt better.

It started when I took responsibility.

I got help.
I got honest.
I built routines.
I asked for support.
I faced my anger instead of feeding it.

Not because I was weak —
Because I was tired of losing.

THE REAL TEACHING

Pain can make you bitter.
Or it can make you built.

But you choose.

REFLECTION

Ask yourself:

- What pain am I using to justify bad habits?
- What behavior am I avoiding taking responsibility for?
- Who would I be if I healed?

<u>Writing space:</u>

_____

_____

_____

_____

_____

_____

_____

_____

_____

_____

_____

_____

_____

_____

20

ACTION CHALLENGE

Today:

Name your pain.

Name your patterns.

Name your accountability partner.

Start healing intentionally.

Your future deserves a healed version of you.

<u>Writing space:</u>

_____

_____

_____

_____

_____

LEGACY KEYS

- Pain is real
- Responsibility is power
- Healing is leadership

- Trauma must be faced
- Your healing protects generations

CHAPTER 4

YOUR CIRCLE IS YOUR FUTURE

You can't outgrow the environment you keep choosing.

You can pray.

You can dream.

You can set goals.

But if your circle stays the same, your future usually does too.

I learned this the hard way.

WHO YOU STAND WITH DETERMINES WHERE YOU STAND

There were people in my life who loved me —
But didn't lead me.

They weren't evil.
They were just unstructured.

They normalized late nights.

They normalized bad money habits.

They normalized chaos, broken relationships, emotional immaturity, and survival mode.

They weren't trying to destroy my life —
But they weren't protecting it either.

And protection matters more than intentions.

THE MOMENT I CHANGED MY CIRCLE

I reached a point where I had to choose:

Keep familiar relationships —
Or protect my future.

That was painful.

But peace always costs something.

I distanced myself from people who didn't respect my goals, my discipline, my healing, or my direction.

Not out of pride.

Out of survival.

And that decision upgraded my entire life.

YOUR CIRCLE MULTIPLIES YOU

Your circle multiplies your habits.

Your mindset.

Your discipline.

Your money behavior.

Your emotional health.

That's why some people stay tired, broke, distracted, and unstable —
Even when they work hard.

Their circle is leaking their future.

REFLECTION

Ask yourself:

• Who challenges your growth?

• Who drains your discipline?

• Who would panic if you actually healed?

Writing space:

_____

_____

_____

_____

_____

_____

_____

_____

_____

_____

_____

_____

_____

_____

ACTION CHALLENGE

Audit your circle:

Reduce exposure to chaos.

Increase exposure to growth.

Choose peace over popularity.

Your future is listening to your relationships.

<u>Writing space:</u>

_____

_____

_____

_____

_____

LEGACY KEYS

- Environment shapes destiny
- Protection beats popularity
- Your circle is your mirror
- Peace is power
- You outgrow some people

CHAPTER 5

REAL LEADERS BUILD, NOT BURN

Some people live to create chaos.

Real leaders live to create stability.

Stability is not boring.

Stability is **protection.**

It protects your mind.

Your money.

Your family.

Your future.

I had to learn that stability is not weakness —

It's leadership.

CHAOS IS EXPENSIVE

I watched people lose:

Jobs.

Homes.

Relationships.

Opportunities.

Freedom.

Not because they were bad —

But because they were unstable.

Late payments.

Bad credit.

No savings.

No plan.

No routine.

Chaos drains your future silently.

BUILDING MY STABILITY SYSTEM

When I finally got serious, I didn't just say "I want better."

I built systems:

• Budget tracking

• Credit rebuilding

• Fitness routines

• Education goals

• Emergency savings

- Boundaries with time
- Spiritual discipline

Those systems gave me peace.

Not luck.

Not miracles.

Structure.

YOUR STABILITY PLAN

You need five pillars:

1. Financial order
2. Physical health
3. Mental discipline
4. Education/skill growth
5. Faith & mindset

These pillars protect you when life hits.

REFLECTION

Ask yourself:

- What area of my life lacks structure?
- What system would immediately improve my peace?

Writing space:

_____

_____

_____

_____

_____

_____

_____

_____

_____

_____

_____

_____

_____

_____

_____

ACTION CHALLENGE

Start your stability system today:

Track your money.

Move your body.

Read 10 pages.

Save something.

Protect your time.

Stability is leadership.

<u>Writing space:</u>

_____

_____

_____

_____

_____

LEGACY KEYS

- Stability is strength
- Structure creates peace
- Systems protect futures
- Leaders build
- Chaos steals quietly

CHAPTER 6

DISCIPLINE IS YOUR SUPERPOWER

Motivation is emotional.

Discipline is structural.

Motivation comes and goes.

Discipline carries you when feelings disappear.

Every stable, successful, peaceful life is built on discipline.

Not hype.

Not luck.

Not talent.

Structure.

WHY MOST PEOPLE STAY STUCK

They wait to "feel like it."

Feel like waking up.

Feel like saving money.

Feel like healing.

Feel like changing.

Discipline says:

We move anyway.

That's how my life changed.

MY DISCIPLINE RESET

When I came out of survival mode, I built daily rules:

Wake up early.

Move my body.

Track my money.

Read something.

Pray/reflect.

Protect my time.

Those weren't "habits."

They were shields.

They protected my mental health, my peace, my growth, and my future.

STRUCTURE BEATS STRESS

Stress increases when structure decreases.

Discipline reduces anxiety because it creates predictability.

Predictability creates peace.

REFLECTION

Ask yourself:

- What am I inconsistent with?
- What would change my life if I did it daily?

Writing space:

_____

_____

_____

_____

_____

_____

_____

_____

_____

_____

_____

_____

ACTION CHALLENGE

Create 3 non-negotiables:

One for your body

One for your money

One for your mind

Do them daily.

<u>Writing space:</u>

_____

_____

_____

_____

_____

LEGACY KEYS

- Discipline protects peace
- Feelings lie
- Structure builds freedom
- Consistency creates confidence
- Your routine writes your future

CHAPTER 7

YOUR NAME IS YOUR BRAND

Your name is not just what people call you.

It's what people *expect* from you.

Your name is your credit score.

Your reputation.

Your access.

Your opportunities.

Your name walks into rooms before you do.

I LEARNED THIS IN REAL LIFE

I've been on both sides of reputation.

I've been the one people didn't trust yet.
And I've been the one people called when they needed
leadership, stability, and solutions.

The difference wasn't luck.

It was consistency.

It was showing up.

Keeping my word.

Protecting my image.

Protecting my habits.

Protecting my circle.

Over time, my name became a key.

YOUR NAME OPENS DOORS

People hire names.

People partner with names.

People protect names.

Your name can open doors —
Or close rooms.

REFLECTION

Ask yourself:

- What does my name currently represent?
- Would people trust my future child with me?

Writing space:

_____

_____

_____

_____

_____

_____

_____

_____

_____

_____

_____

_____

_____

_____

_____

ACTION CHALLENGE

Protect your name:

Be early.

Keep your word.

Handle your money.

Treat people well.

Stay consistent.

Your name is your brand.

<u>Writing space:</u>

_____

_____

_____

_____

_____

LEGACY KEYS

- Reputation is currency
- Trust is power
- Consistency builds names
- Your name writes your access
- Protect your brand

CHAPTER 8

YOU WERE BORN TO BREAK CYCLES

Some people live for today.

Leaders live for generations.

Your decisions don't stop with you.

They echo.

They travel through families, children, and futures.

I had to realize I wasn't just fixing *my* life —

I was correcting a bloodline.

THE CYCLES I SAW

I saw cycles of:

Poverty

Absent fathers

Incarceration

Addiction

Emotional instability

Hopelessness

They weren't accidents.

They were inherited systems.

And systems must be **replaced**, not just avoided.

BECOMING THE INTERRUPTION

Breaking cycles isn't emotional — it's structural.

It's budgets.

It's boundaries.

It's discipline.

It's education.

It's healing.

I chose to become the interruption.

Not perfect.

But intentional.

REFLECTION

Ask yourself:

- What cycle stops with me?
- What cycle starts with me?

Writing space:

_____

_____

_____

_____

_____

_____

_____

_____

_____

_____

_____

_____

_____

_____

ACTION CHALLENGE

Build one system that didn't exist in your family:

Savings.

Healthy routines.

Education habits.

Healing conversations.

Be the blueprint.

Writing space:

_____

_____

_____

_____

_____

LEGACY KEYS

- Cycles are broken intentionally
- Systems create new futures
- Healing changes generations
- You are the interruption
- Build what you never had

CHAPTER 10

YOUR NEXT DECISION MATTERS

You don't need perfection.

You need direction.

Your life does not change all at once.

It changes **one decision at a time.**

And the next one matters more than you think.

THE TRUTH ABOUT CHANGE

People wait for the "right time."

But the right time is always now.

I didn't rebuild my life with big speeches.

I rebuilt it with small decisions repeated daily.

Earlier mornings.

Better boundaries.

Healthier habits.

Smarter money moves.

More intentional relationships.

That's how stability is built.

YOU ARE ONE DECISION AWAY

One decision can:

Change your health

Change your future

Change your children

Change your peace

Change your legacy

One.

REFLECTION

Ask yourself:

- What decision would improve my life immediately?
- What decision have I been delaying?

<u>Writing space:</u>

_____

_____

_____

_____

_____

_____

_____

_____

_____

_____

_____

_____

_____

_____

ACTION CHALLENGE

Today:

Do the hard thing.

Start the habit.

Send the email.

Set the boundary.

Choose peace.

Your next decision writes your future.

Writing space:

_____

_____

_____

_____

_____

LEGACY KEYS

• Direction beats perfection

• Small decisions build big lives

• Today shapes tomorrow

• You are one choice away

• Choose wisely

This book was never about motivation. It was about direction. It was about giving people who grew up without a blueprint the systems, structure, and language to rebuild their lives with intention. Everything written here comes from lived experience—mistakes made, losses faced, healing chosen, and stability built. The truth is, no one accidentally becomes strong, stable, disciplined, or healed. Those outcomes are the result of daily decisions repeated over time. You do not drift into peace. You decide your way into it.

Every chapter has shown one core truth: your life moves in the direction of your choices. Your habits, your circle, your discipline, your boundaries, and your healing all write your future before it arrives. You are not broken—you are becoming. And becoming requires intention. It requires accountability. It requires the courage to choose structure over chaos and purpose over pain. You are not late. You are not behind. You are simply one decision away from a different future.

So today, make this commitment to yourself: I will choose growth over familiarity. I will choose healing over hiding. I will choose discipline over excuses. I will choose structure over chaos. I will protect my name, my future, and my bloodline. I understand that age does not make me grown— my decisions do. And starting today, I choose to build a life that the next generation can stand on.

FINAL COMMITMENT & LEGACY PLEDGE

This book was never meant to sit on a shelf. It was written to sit inside your life.

Every page you have read was built from real choices, real losses, real healing, and real rebuilding. This blueprint exists because you deserve more than survival—you deserve structure, stability, peace, and purpose. Your life is not random. Your future is not accidental. You are becoming the result of your decisions, whether you realize it or not.

Today, you are invited to make a conscious commitment to yourself and the generations connected to you.

Read this out loud:

I commit to choosing growth over familiarity.
I commit to choosing healing over hiding.
I commit to choosing discipline over excuses.
I commit to choosing structure over chaos.
I commit to protecting my name, my future, and my bloodline.

I understand that age does not make me grown—my decisions do.

And starting today, I choose to build a life that the next generation can stand on.

Sign your name below, because this is no longer just a book—it is your blueprint.

Name: _____

Date: _____

AUTHOR & PROGRAM INFORMATION

Larry D. Wilcox

Founder — Turn It Up Leadership Group

Cleveland, Ohio

Larry D. Wilcox is a U.S. Army combat veteran, community leader, and nationally recognized youth mentor dedicated to helping individuals build stability, discipline, and purpose through intentional decision-making and life-structure systems.

Turn It Up Leadership Group is a leadership development and life-stability organization that provides mentorship programs, social-emotional learning workshops, re-entry support, and personal development training for youth and adults. The organization specializes in breaking generational cycles, strengthening decision-making skills, and building long-term stability in underserved communities.

For speaking engagements, school partnerships, workshops, and program inquiries:

Email: Turnitupspeakig@gmail.com

www.ingramcontent.com/pod-product-compliance
Lightning Source LLC
Chambersburg PA
CBHW051557120626
46551CB00013B/1553